How to get Into a Woman's Knickers

By

RON HOKELBY

Order this book online at www.trafford.com/07-1716
or email orders@trafford.com

Most Trafford titles are also available at major online book retailers.

Note for Librarians: A cataloguing record for this book is available from Library and Archives Canada at www.collectionscanada.ca/amicus/index-e.html

ISBN: 978-1-4251-4156-1

We at Trafford believe that it is the responsibility of us all, as both individuals and corporations, to make choices that are environmentally and socially sound. You, in turn, are supporting this responsible conduct each time you purchase a Trafford book, or make use of our publishing services. To find out how you are helping, please visit www.trafford.com/responsiblepublishing.html

Our mission is to efficiently provide the world's finest, most comprehensive book publishing service, enabling every author to experience success. To find out how to publish your book, your way, and have it available worldwide, visit us online at www.trafford.com/10510

www.trafford.com

North America & international
toll-free: 1 888 232 4444 (USA & Canada)
phone: 250 383 6864 ♦ fax: 250 383 6804
email: info@trafford.com

The United Kingdom & Europe
phone: +44 (0)1865 722 113 ♦ local rate: 0845 230 9601
facsimile: +44 (0)1865 722 868 ♦ email: info.uk@trafford.com

10 9 8 7 6 5 4 3 2

Contents

Introduction 7
About the author 11
Chapter 1 Learn the knowledge 13
Chapter 2 Women think we're stupid17
Chapter 3 Looks don't matter 21
Chapter 4 No need for small talk. . . .25
Chapter 5 Do you need to be rich . . .29
Chapter 6 No flashy clothes 33
Chapter 7 Does age matter. 37
Chapter 8 Do I need a sporty car. . . .39
Chapter 9 Where do you go 43
Chapter 10 Get back. 47
Chapter 11 The four golden steps 49

Introduction

Before you read this book, you must know that previous to having the knowledge that I now have, I failed so many times. I was a fallen man, my efforts were ridiculous. But now my confidence is so high. I follow my 4 - step rule all the time and I never fail. Yes you read correctly I NEVER FAIL. This is a 100% guaranteed step by step guide to getting into a woman's knickers. There is no quicker fix than a quick fix, but you must be patient. Take your time and read this

book in the correct order. After all, your failure rate more than likely overshadows your success rate.

Good luck
Ron Hokelby

About the author

Ron Hokelby spent one year studying for a physiology diploma before realizing a common sense diploma in life is all you need to get by. Married with 3 children, he plans to climb Mount Everest next Wednesday before lunch, as he has a prior appointment at the chiropodist in the afternoon. This book follows his two unpublished books "I'm a millionaire and yes I am happy" and "How to boil an egg in a wetsuit".

Chapter 1
Learn the knowledge

How many times have you been driving to work, another dull, boring day ahead of you and you suddenly spot this cracker coming towards you ? Jesus I'd love to get into her knickers, you say to yourself. You sit there ogling, eyes popping out of your head but you do nothing about it. Why? Lack of confidence - maybe you're a little shy. Maybe you feel you don't have the know

how. Well, believe or not, you do, its just you need something to trigger it all off for you. Well that something is in your hands now. This book will show you in 4 golden steps how to get into girls knickers effortlessly.

You could rush to chapter 10 now and find the solution. That would be the quick fix, the lazy way. My advice is to slowly read chapters 1 - 9 and you will learn more. After all you've been trying for years, failure after failure. What's another hour or so going to matter to you.

Chapter 2
Women think we're stupid

Most women have said at least once in their lives that they think men are stupid. Even your own mother has said it about you at one stage or another. Remember the time you were running back from the ice - cream van, all excited, tongue hanging out like a demented horse. Are we talking about the same time ? Yes, the time you dropped the little bouquet of vanilla cones. What

were you called ? Yes, stupid, along with another few choice words

As you grow up, you meet a girl or two, then you meet that special one. You think she thinks your super. Well surprise , surprise - as your woman with the big teeth on the telly used to say - when she gets together with her mates, they have they're little girlie chats. Eventually the super boyfriends come into the conversation. "Oh my John, -that's you- he can be so thick sometimes"

It's the same when you marry your lovely wife. The plumber comes to fix the leak or the carpenter to fix the lock. She makes him coffee and says what a great job he's doing, and oh yes, how quick he is because " you know my Johnny would be hours doing that he's hopeless, he can't do anything"

Well you're far from hopeless and definitely not stupid. Soon you'll know the 4 golden steps. Soon you can show them who the stupid one is.

Chapter 3
Looks don't matter

You've showered, shaved, sprayed, you look at yourself in the mirror. That big nose is staring back at you. Those pointy spock ears seem to be getting bigger. You squeeze those spots a bit much and you've red blotches all over your face. The more you look at yourself the bigger your eyebrows seem to be getting. "I should have let my locks grow like Brad".

He always gets the girls.

Well believe it or not none of this matters. I will prove to you that you don't need to shower. You don't need deodorant. Grow a beard down to your knees if you want. If you really want, let some snot roll on to your lip and wipe it across your face with your sleeve. Just for good measure part your hair at the side and flatten it down with custard instead of wax or gel.

Even with this new look you'll be a success, believe me.

Chapter 4
No need for small talk

Johnny gets on great with the women. "Ah yeah" but sure isn't Johnny hilarious. He's got all the one liners. He knows all the chat up lines. Johnny has a success rate second to none. Well, now you can say to Johnny " You know all your little ice - breakers Johnny, you wouldn't mind shoving them up your **** would you". Because with my method you don't need to open your mouth except

to breathe. And even then, with your big nose , you probably don't use your mouth for breathing. This is your chance to put Johnny in the shade. No more writing jokes on the inside of your cigarette box. No more rehearsing in your best Joey voice "How you doing". Believe me, this is so easy Johnny might end up looking up to YOU after this.

Chapter 5
Do you need to be rich

I must admit when I discovered this technique I had a small sum in the bank. But taking into consideration my loans and outgoings I wasn't exactly loaded.

Using this technique, if you got a plain white t-shirt and using a black marker wrote, "I'M BROKE AND HAVEN'T A POT TO PISS IN" you will be as successful if not more of a success than Pierce in accounts. Who does he think he is buying everybody

drinks with his platinum credit card.

You don't need to be rich. You don't need five different credit cards. I estimate to carry out the steps in this book, you will not have to spend anymore than the price of a big Mac meal. You don't need to slide up to a girl and offer to buy her a drink and another and another. Listen Spotty, you don't need to get anyone drunk anymore including yourself. Just follow the 4 golden steps.

Chapter 6
No flashy clothes

On with the designer jeans, your lucky shirt and clean up those shoes or boots. I think I'll just carry my jacket to-night, I might crease my lucky shirt. How lucky is it really. You've been out fifty times, you had a result once. If you were a horse they'd have had you destroyed. You would have been just as popular in a sack with holes cut out for the arms. Before I discovered this

technique I used to try. Not anymore. I'm the one at the bar with the custard in my hair, remember?. A cave - man could have a 100% success rate with this method.

Why try too hard if you don't have to. Let Johnny spend two hours getting ready. Close your eyes next time you go to your wardrobe and grab anything. During research I bought a top and corduroy trousers from a charity shop for less than the price of a pint of milk.If you want I'll swap them for your lucky shirt. The bottom line is you don't need flashy clothes.

Chapter 7
Does age matter

A man of fifty will have a success rate on par with a twenty year old. Age is not a barrier. That seventy six year old man with the walking stick, now he'd be a little bit slower but he will reach his goal. But remember this is not a race and the four golden steps never discriminate against age.

Chapter 8
Do I need a sporty car

"I must say they're really popular with the women" said the car salesman. But then he would, he'd say anything to get you to part with your hard earned cash. Car salesmen, the only people to go into fits of laughter when you tell them your worst joke. They just want one thing, your money. You leave the showroom thinking you're the funniest bloke in the world. You could be a very successful stand-

up according to his reaction.

You have your flashy motor now, now for the real test. You pull up at the lights, what a piece of good fortune, she's just pulled up beside you. You look over, tapping the steering wheel to some stupid song on the radio. Finally she looks over, she looks at your passion wagon, looks at the traffic lights and vroom she's gone. Lets break it down.

You're at the lights for 15 seconds. She looks at Flash Harry for 1 second, the lights for 2 seconds and her nails for the remainder. You weren't very successful were you. You don't need a flash car. That smarmy car salesman made a nice bit of commission for himself didn't he. Still feeling hilarious are we.

Chapter 9
Where do you go

There are lots of ways to meet women. A pub, a club, a blind date or speed dating to name a few. Some people are successful here but it's hard work.

Try an internet dating service for example. My name is Moses, I'm 8 foot 12 inches tall, look like the elephant man and smell like Parmesan cheese. I've 6 toes on one foot and the other one is webbed. I need a girl who can understand me when

I have an apple jammed in my mouth and a carrot stuck up either nostril.

I guarantee a match or two will be found for you but unfortunately she doesn't exist - like Moses - or she's Moses sister.

You don't need to frequent pubs, clubs or the like . You just need the formula and your holy grail awaits.

Skip chapter 10 if you're the patient type as described in chapter 1. If your not you've read it already.

Chapter 10
Get back

Get back to chapter 2 and have patience for once in your life. It's the best way, you know it is. Go on.

Chapter 11
The four golden steps

You are finally here. Your journey is nearly over. It's quite simple just follow the four steps in order. Don't rush your self and remember practise makes perfect.

You'll need a pen and paper for this as it's written backwards for the impatient people.

Step 1
teg flesruoy a riap fo s'nemow srekcink.
Step 2
tup ruoy tfel gel ni.
Step 3
won ruoy thgir gel.
Step 4
llup meht pu.

Congratulations, another success story, well done.

www.ingramcontent.com/pod-product-compliance
Ingram Content Group UK Ltd.
Pitfield, Milton Keynes, MK11 3LW, UK
UKHW020137250726
13967UKWH00002B/714

9 781425 141561